ONTARIO

ONTARIO

A BICENTENNIAL TRIBUTE

KEY PORTER BOOKS

Copyright © 1983 Key Porter Books
All Rights Reserved

Key Porter Books
59 Front Street East
Toronto M5E 1B3

Canadian Cataloguing in Publication Data
Main entry under title:
Ontario: a bicentennial tribute

ISBN 0-919493-17-3

1. Ontario   2. Ontario - Centennial celebrations, etc.

FC3061.O57   1983   971.3   C83-098997-8
F1057.O57   1983

Designed by Gerry Takeuchi
Printed and bound in Ontario

Acknowledgements

The following poem is used by permission of The House of Anansi Press Ltd., Toronto: "400: Coming Home" from *Civil Elegies and Other Poems*, by Dennis Lee. The following excerpt is used by permission of the author: "The Algoma Hills" from *A Broken Journey*, by Morley Callaghan.
The following excerpts and poems are used by permission of The Canadian Publishers, McClelland and Stewart Ltd., Toronto: "North of Superior" from *The Collected Poems*, by Earle Birney, "Canoe: the Exacting Servant" from *A Supersonic Day*, by Gregory Clark, "The Path of Life" from *Ojibway Ceremonies*, by Basil Johnston, "Mariposa" from *Sunshine Sketches of a Little Town*, by Stephen Leacock, "The Country of the Young" from *Purdy Selected*, by Al Purdy.

Captions for Preliminary Pages

(*Page 2*) Toronto's famous landmark, the CN Tower stands glittering above the city at night. The Tower is the world's tallest free-standing structure at 553 metres, and besides a magnificent view and rotating restaurant, provides some of the most efficient facilities in the world for radio and television transmission.

(*Page 5*) A bright autumn day at Bridal Veil Falls near Canyon Station in the magnificent Northern Ontario Agawa Canyon.

(*Page 6*) Winter sledding in Toronto's High Park.

PHOTO CREDITS

Mary Abbott
pages 26 (bottom), 29 (top).

Paul von Baich
pages 21 (top), 34 (bottom), 37 (top), 40-41, 42 (top), 45 (bottom), 65 (top), 68 (top, middle and bottom), 69, 70 (top), 85 (top), 107 (bottom), 116 (bottom), 146 (top), 147.

Alan Baker
pages 24, 61 (top).

Courtesy of Carling Bassett
page 143 (bottom).

Courtesy of Bell Canada
page 97.

Courtesy of Salome Bey
page 154.

Courtesy of the Canadian Opera Company
(photo by Robert Ragsdale) page 159 (bottom)

Harry Dahme
pages 26 (top), 29 (bottom), 37 (bottom), 62-63.

Gera Dillon
pages 20, 21 (bottom), 60 (top), 64, 83 (right), 86 (top), 111 (bottom), 145 (top).

Courtesy of Dome Mines Ltd.
page 113 (top).

Don Eldon
pages 22 (top), 30 (top).

Ken Elliott
pages 30 (bottom), 48, 70 (bottom), 71 (top), 88, 116 (top), 119 (top).

Courtesy of General Motors of Canada
page 113 (middle left).

Courtesy of the Hospital for Sick Children
(photo by Lou Scagleone): page 60 (bottom left).

George Hunter
pages 5, 17, 22 (bottom), 25 (bottom), 31, 32-33, 35 (bottom), 58, 85 (bottom), 98-99, 103 (top), 106 (top and bottom), 108-109, 110, 112, 118 (bottom), 119 (bottom), 134 (bottom), 146 (bottom).

Jack Jarvie
pages 44, 65 (bottom), 73 (middle), 76 (bottom), 77, 116 (middle), 151 (top).

Lois and Brian King
pages 18-19, 39 (bottom), 43 (bottom right), 87, 104, 113 (bottom), 114-115, 117 (top), 118 (top).

Courtesy of the McLaughlin Planetarium, Royal Ontario Museum
page 152 (bottom).

Edward Meyer
page 61 (middle).

Courtesy of the National Ballet of Canada
pages 156-157

Paul Newberry
pages 25 (top), 27.

John O'Brien
pages 23, 36, 45 (top), 59 (bottom), 61 (bottom), 101 (left), 103 (bottom), 117 (bottom), 132, 148-149, 155 (left).

Courtesy of Ontario Hydro
pages 105 (bottom), 111 (top).

Courtesy of the Ontario Science Centre
page 152 (top).

Courtesy of Parks Canada
pages 43 (top), 46 (top).

Roberto Portolese
pages 2, 42 (bottom), 46 (bottom left), 59 (top), 80 (bottom), 81, 82.

Barry Ranford
pages 34 (top), 35 (top).

Courtesy of the Shaw Festival
page 158.

Bill Smith
page 155 (right).

Fiona Spalding-Smith
pages 100 (top), 130-131, 136-137.

Courtesy of Spar Aerospace Ltd.
page 102.

Boris Spremo
pages 83 (left), 105 (top), 134 (top), 138 (bottom), 140-141, 143 (top), 144, 150, 151 (middle and bottom).

Courtesy of the Toronto Blue Jays
page 142.

Courtesy of the Toronto Stock Exchange
page 100 (bottom).

John de Visser
pages 8, 28, 38, 39 (top), 43 (bottom left), 45 (middle), 46 (bottom right), 47, 57, 60 (bottom right), 67 (top), 71 (bottom), 72, 74-75, 84 (top and bottom), 101 (right), 113 (middle right), 133 (bottom), 135, 153.

Ron Watts
pages 6, 66, 67 (bottom right and left), 76 (top), 80 (top), 86 (bottom), 107 (top), 120, 129, 133 (top), 138 (top), 139 (top and bottom), 159 (top), 160.

John Williamson
pages 73 (top and bottom), 78 (top and bottom), 79, 145 (bottom).

TABLE OF CONTENTS

LEGACIES

In the Beginning

William Kilbourn

They were refugees and defeated soldiers, the settlers of 1784, looking for land and work and peace in what was left of British North America.

Among the American colonists who eventually found their way to the virgin forests of Ontario, there were a few well-to-do tories like the Robinsons of Virginia, persecuted for their loyalty by the revolutionary mobs; there were pacifists like the Mennonites and Quakers of Pennsylvania; but the great majority of that first six thousand who occupied the banks of the St. Lawrence and the Niagara and the Kingston-to-Quinte shore were simple farmers who had been on the losing side of what was essentially a New York civil war.

The old regiments were kept together: Colonel Butler's Rangers at Newark, Major Rogers' Corps west of Fort Cataraqui and Sir John Johnson's Royal Yorkers – Anglicans, Scottish Presbyterians, Gaelic-speaking Catholic Highlanders, German Lutherans and German Calvinists, each in their separate allotments – from Longueil to the Long Sault to the Thousand Islands.

To defend themselves against the assault of the seasons in their new homeland, they were each supplied by the British authorities with axe and saw, hammer, pick and crowbar, carpenter's tools, hoes, twine, ploughshares, seed and a few provisions. Land grants ranged from fifty acres for an ordinary civilian to two hundred for NCOs and a thousand for field officers. Some brought wives and children and animals, a few had servants and heirlooms.

The necessary land was purchased from the Mississaugas and other aboriginal peoples, including three million acres for the British allies Joseph Brant and the Six Nations to make their new home on the banks of the Grand.

Until then, the Great Lakes region had been the domain of a few migrant tribes, the merchants and *coureurs de bois* who traded with them, and a sparse scattering of soldiers whose palisades and plumage symbolized the suzerainty of a European monarch.

The only settlements of any size in what is now Ontario were at the two extremities: the *habitants* placed along the river banks at Fort Detroit in the last years of the French regime, and the hive of storekeepers and craftsmen who had occupied the main Hudson's Bay Company post on the Moose River south of James Bay since the 17th century.

In 1791 the Loyalists were granted British institutions and laws in the new colony of Upper Canada. Expecting another American war, Governor Simcoe chose the protected harbour of Toronto for the site of a fort and his capital. He and his wife Elizabeth lived in a tent purchased from the effects of the explorer Captain Cook and, like Adam and Eve new-naming things in the Garden, set about creating a society.

(*Left*) Carved by the Algonquin Indians over a thousand years ago, these ancient petroglyphs near Peterborough are part of the largest concentrations of Indian rock inscriptions in North America. Despite careful study by archeologists, their meaning remains a tantalizing mystery.

Simcoe's British officials stayed on to become, along with a few educated Loyalists, the colony's governing class. Their children's tutor, John Strachan, who sailed from Scotland to New York in 1799, and thence walked through the forest to Kingston, became their spokesman during the American invasion of 1813, and after the war their political leader. George III, he told them, though he had never been to England, was a paragon of men and that democrat Jefferson the devil incarnate.

Strachan became the first bishop of Toronto but his goal was to "preach civilization" as well as the Gospel. The father of education in the province, he also created the Loyalist myth and guarded against the incursion of American democracy.

Upper Canada was in the path of the American migration west, however, and by 1812 the population was predominately American. My ancestors crossed the Niagara River in 1794, to take up land in what is now London, and like most of their fellows, they were scarcely aware of being under a new allegiance and little inclined to serve a governing class. Their spokesman was another poor Scottish immigrant, the populist editor and agitator William Lyon Mackenzie. He eventually led them in an armed uprising, whose final defeat was planned in Strachan's parlour.

The upshot of 1837 was that neither opponent was to dominate again. Their ideals interfered with progress and prosperity. But they are still our best spiritual guides. Like the lion and the unicorn contending for the Crown, tory Strachan and radical Mackenzie are fixed forever in the still-motion dance of the monarch's Coat of Arms, augury and emblem of this royal province of the pioneers.

The Royal Ontario Museum

Margaret Atwood

When I was ten, in 1947 or so, I used to spend Saturday mornings at the Royal Ontario Museum. I was attending an art class, of sort. We were taken in groups to sit on fold-up wooden stools in front of something which would be expounded to us: a suit of armour, a stuffed animal, a stone Peruvian god. Then we would go to the cellar and do artistic things with whatever materials were provided. I remember tempera paint, feathers, glue, buttons, cloth and wool, and the odd smell of the surroundings, a little like church only with more bouquet.

The best part came afterwards. I had a friend who also went to these classes, and whose father worked at the Museum. The arrangement was that we would meet him at his office and he would drive us home; but we always took a long time getting there. We ranged freely throughout the Museum, dodging the custodians, exploring, with the exciting sense that we were doing something that was not forbidden only because it had not yet been detected.

The Museum was less frequented on Saturdays than it is now, and the space seemed endless, labyrinthine, empty of living people, populated by statues and gods and clothing worn by invisible people, and strewn with the kinds of things I had otherwise encountered only in adventure stories: crossbows, blowpipes, necklaces dug up from tombs, cave bears, skulls. Our favourites were, of course, the Egyptian mummies, which we approached with queasy and delicious fear – would they start to move? – and the dinosaurs, which on the contrary we thought of as potential though overgrown pets. In those days, the

Museum's superb Oriental collections were just places you had to go past on your way to the real stuff. Coming out afterwards, onto Avenue Road, into the usually grey and chilly Toronto weather, was always a let-down: after all that colour and drama and time-travel, daylight and chicken noodle soup for lunch were slightly flat.

Since then, the R.O.M. has remained for me the prototype of museums. I don't find a museum truly satisfactory and complete unless it has a totem pole up the central staircase, a Tyrannosaurus Rex, a glass case containing a prehistoric Egyptian sand burial. I had no idea when I was younger that this museum was exceptional in any way: weren't they all just like it? I have since discovered that they aren't – that some have more of this or that, many less, but that few offer the variety and that quality of something akin to eccentricity that the R.O.M. should take care not to streamline out of existence completely. (The paleontologist in his cage, looking like something the sabre-toothed tigers dragged in, the sabre-toothed tigers themselves, fake as can be, sinking eternally into their black paint tar pit. . . .)

And beside the Museum is that other dimension of space-time, the Planetarium. Here, in a darkness permeated with the smell of bubble gum and punctuated by the soft thud of schoolchildren digging each other in the ribs with their elbows, you can lie back as if at the hairdresser's and watch outer space unreel itself backwards and forwards, while a voice like a cross between God's and a used car salesman's explains the inexplicable. There's nothing more relaxing than to feel yourself dwindling, not merely to a footprint in the sands of time, but to a gentle smudge.

Many cities expand outward; Toronto expands inward as well: you go in to get out, of this place, of this world.

The R.O.M. is essence of museum, the quintessential time capsule. I never learn much in it in any systematic way. I don't read the fine print on the labels. I go there to roll around in the past, like a pig in mud. It's still total immersion.

The One-Party Province

Robert Fulford

The most striking fact about politics in Ontario is now so familiar that few of us remark on it: Ontario is apparently a one-party state. Since 1905, the Conservatives (renamed the Progressive Conservatives in 1942) have governed Ontario most of the time, and since 1943 they have governed *all* of the time. To the continued dismay of their opponents, they have won all the elections, and today most people have lived only under Conservative premiers. In the history of party politics in the western democracies, no other party has governed so large a place for so long.

The Conservatives have achieved this by being infinitely flexible, bending and changing as the province has changed, and by at least appearing to renew themselves with each new leader. At the end of the Second World War they seemed an ordinary conservative party, like any other in the Western world – opposed to heavy government spending, determined to put a brake on taxation and bureaucracy, in favour of private enterprise and (so far as government could impose one) a strict moral code. Forty years later they resemble in many ways a social democratic government. They have presided over a gigantic increase in government spending and the bureaucracy. They have enlarged enormously educational services (so that post-secondary education of some kind is available to almost every young resident of the province), and they have organized (along with the federal government) a system of universal health care. They are heavily involved in industrial strategy and even in the arts. They have in fact done just about everything that the Conservatives of the 1940s said shouldn't be done. And they have done it without leaving office for one minute.

The four premiers from 1943 to 1983 are all describable in roughly the same demographic terms – male Anglo-Saxon Protestant lawyers from small (or, in one case, medium-sized) cities. But they have differed, and the differences reflect the life of Ontario over forty years.

The first, George Drew, in the 1940s, represented the pro-British Ontario of the war-time period. A former soldier himself, he looked and spoke like a proud British military officer sent out to govern a colony. He vehemently opposed the Liberal government in Ottawa (which he criticized, among other things, for incompetently pursuing the war effort and for softness toward communism). In 1948 he moved to Ottawa, to national leadership of the party, and to failure.

His successor, Leslie Frost, was a comfortable, never strident leader, altogether suited to the relaxed and prosperous Ontario of the 1950s. Unlike Drew, Frost got on well with Ottawa; he began that process by which Conservative Ontario governments and Liberal Ottawa governments increasingly saw eye to eye, a process which in recent years has produced a degree of fury west of the Lakehead.

Frost gave way to John Robarts, a figure of great apparent bonhomie, who exuded an air of high-level boardroom competence. Ontario was now becoming more sophisticated, and its old-fashioned laws (such as those governing liquor) were slowly being relaxed. Robarts presided over the professionalization of the civil service (he learned more than a little from Jean Lesage's Quebec) and made Ontario a more committed partner in Confederation. By then immigration was transforming life in Ontario, and Robarts recognized this change. He brought to an end, at least in public, the antagonism between Ontario and Quebec, an antagonism based to a large extent on ancient blood feuds between English and French and between Protestants and Catholics. This was not a moment too soon: during the career of Robarts' successor Toronto was to become more Catholic than Protestant. There was no longer any serious public support for Protestant-rooted politics.

Robarts' successor turned out to be William Davis, who as education minister rode to fame on the education boom of the 1960s. Like earlier Tory premiers, Davis has relied for his success on the fact that his opposition is seriously split. The Liberals and the New Democrats dislike each other more than they dislike the Tories and there has never been any serious proposal to unite them in opposition. Anti-Conservative votes may at times outweigh pro-Conservative votes, but the Conservatives win more seats and usually a majority.

But much more than this historic piece of luck has kept Davis in office. He has proved a master tactician, managing simultaneously to maintain the faith of old-fashioned conservatives while appearing flexible enough to attract others. His government has been more progressive than conservative, to the point where right-wing journalists often accuse it of despotic socialism. Like Leslie Frost, Davis has made a delicate peace with the Liberals in Ottawa and restrained his enthusiasm for the leadership of the national party.

Seen over forty years, the change in the party is radical and almost magical. Seen in the short term, in day-to-day decisions, it is so slow as to be almost invisible. The government of Ontario moves like a glacier, but it moves.

Franco-Ontario

June Callwood

The province is two hundred years old, but not as Belle River reckons time. People in that small village on Lake St. Clair, a good bicycle ride east of Windsor, are Franco-Ontarians who trace their line for more than a century before the Simcoes put up their tent.

In summer, wild roses grow against the old frame houses of Belle River. Children wade against the placid waves of the shallow lake, the sand a washboard under their feet, the beach behind them littered with the supplicant hands of clam shells. Across from the lumberyard is the home of my great-grandparents, the tiny Sauvés. My grandfather, William Lavoie, lived in an eccentric stone house on the main street. In his parlour an elk head with glassy eyes faced the mournful sepia photograph of my uncle Norval, a child who was drowned in the lake when he was eleven.

Children of Belle River play hide-and-seek in the fragrant dusk, scattering indignant frogs. The language is Frenglish: "*Je te vois! Home free!*"

Growing up in Belle River, my father's English-speaking family pillars of the Anglican church in nearby Tilbury, my mother's French-speaking people reverent at Mass, I lived in the palm of a miracle. I belonged to both. Whatever bitter adjustments had been made by my ancestors did not fall on me. I thought all children had one set of old people who spoke no English and another who spoke no French. It didn't matter, since both were a soft touch for homemade ice cream with shivers of ice in it.

The accommodations of the 18th century, when bloody-minded French and English came reluctantly to the conclusion that genocide was either impractical or impossible, created what is known now as the Canadian mosaic. The groundwork for the peculiarity of ethnic integrity within a larger vision was laid when the founders confronted the reality of a stubborn Belle River. The mosaic lacks the unifying ecstasy of patriotic commitment that distinguishes the American melting pot, but it is a wondrous construction.

It permits uniqueness and intensity. In Ontario people who celebrate the victory of an Italian soccer team are not seen as disloyal to the Canadian flag. Five hundred bagpipes on the green is a Canadian spectacle, and so is a red silk dragon borne by fifty legs.

The pieces which hold their shapes can collide in times of pressure, inflicting pain, but the awesome truth is that more often the contraption works. Playgrounds are filled with children who shout in twenty languages and understand one another. Five friends lunching together can come from five continents.

Ontario learned how to do that long ago. Belle River is the sweet evidence of a good process.

Canoe: the Exacting Servant

Gregory Clark

An acquaintance who very nearly lost a precious twelve-year-old child by drowning wants a warning published about the vicious, treacherous canoe.

The canoe is not, of course, either vicious or treacherous. With the wheel, the loom, and a few other things, it is one of the most valuable of human inventions. I don't know how Europe or Asia were explored, but it was the canoe that opened up the vast wealth and beauty of America. And the bark canoe, at that. A canoe very like the article you buy in the stores today. We must all admit that it was the French Canadians, equipped with the birch-bark canoe of the northern Indians, in all sizes from fifteen feet to forty feet in length, who first explored the great West and down the Mississippi.

The canoe is beautiful, manageable, portable, a work of art. Nobody should be allowed to enter a canoe until willing and able not merely to paddle it, but to lift it from the water to its resting place on shore, rather than drag it up as if it were a keeled boat. If they are not old enough to understand they must treat it as a fragile thing of beauty, to be cared for, to be lifted, to be guarded from bumping into docks, rocks, snags, boulders, to be coddled and cared for, they are not old enough to be allowed to use it.

The boy of twelve to whom I referred above had no more right to be alone in a canoe than in a sports car going fifty miles an hour. The Indians who invented the canoe never paddled more than a few yards from shore even on calm days. If an Indian had to get across a lake a mile wide, he would paddle three miles around its shore. The tremendous journeys the Indians and voyageurs made up the St. Lawrence, through the hundreds of miles of the Great Lakes and up through continuations of the Great Lakes far across the northwest, were all made hugging the shore. And they were interrupted for days at a time when the water was too rough along those shores. Champlain's journals and the Jesuit Relations bear this fact out.

To this day, Indians and woodsmen can always spot a greenhorn in the wilds when they see a canoe in the middle of a lake or river.

"Besides," say the Indians, "what is to be seen far out from the shore? Just water. It is close along the shore that everything of interest is to be found. There is more wisdom in one mile of shore than in ten miles of bush or a hundred miles of water."

So, for all the reasons we can think of, a good canoeman is the along-the-shore man.

Sir Casimir Gzowski

Peter Gzowski

If I walk, as I like to do, across Highway 7 from the small stone house that has become my refuge in the village of Rockwood, I come quite soon to a large barn atop one of Wellington County's comfortably rolling hills. The barn is stone, too. Its walls, like the walls of my house, are of granite that was blasted and cut from the old quarry on my side of the highway. It is almost square, and vast; its dark, cool interior would make a good rock-and-roll recording studio. There is a fireplace in its stable, and stern parapets on its lofty gables. The barn is a fine sight, more than a century old and, as I stand in the shade it offers from the morning sunlight, I am moved by it.

The man who designed the stone barn for an early Wellington County aristocrat with the Dickensian name of Squire Strange was my great-great-grandfather, Casimir Stanislaus Gzowski. Although local records are murky, my supposition is that he did it as something of a favour. Gzowski, who lived at various times in London and Toronto, would have been in the area at the time anyway, laying out and building parts of the Grand Trunk Railway. Gzowski and Strange would have been friends – I assume he is the same Dr. Strange, M.P., who appears on the list of those invited to the founding meeting of the Ontario Jockey Club, which Gzowski also engineered. And, as if in part payment, there is a Gzowski Street in Rockwood, on lands the squire once controlled. In the shadow of the barn, I wonder what my great-great-grandfather must have been like.

He came to Canada an exile. He was the son of a Polish count, born in 1813 and raised, educated and trained as an engineer as part of a generation that was discovering Polish nationalism. In the rebellion of 1830 he fought against the czar, was defeated, imprisoned, sent to Austria and, eventually, to North America. He could speak four languages when he arrived here, but not English. To make up that deficit, he apprenticed himself to a lawyer in Pittsfield, Massachusetts, and supported himself by teaching fencing and horsemanship to the students of a local school for young ladies, one of whom he eventually married. He set to work on the Erie Canal. On a business excursion to Upper Canada, his presence was brought to the attention of the governor, Sir Charles Bagot. Bagot had known Gzowski's father at the czar's court in St. Petersburg. He offered Gzowski a job in roads and waterways.

His mark, now, is imprinted on the province. He built the first bridge across the Niagara River – an engineering marvel. He paved and extended Yonge Street. He built much of the Grand Trunk. Everywhere, there are bridges, or stretches of highway or railway that display his style. His bust presides over the Niagara Parks Commission and a park in Toronto honours his name and memory.

In his later years, he became a distinguished figure in the province's society, in one way or another directing or influencing the fortunes of the Philharmonic Society, Wycliffe College, the Dominion Rifle Association, the Jockey Club, various engineering associations and the Conservative Party. When Sir John A. Macdonald left office, Gzowski headed the committee of businessmen who raised the necessary retirement fund. In 1880, Queen Victoria knighted him and named him her colonial aide-de-camp in Canada. In a different age, when his tongue-twisting name and formal, accented English would have been less noticeable, he might have reached even more prominence.

He kept no diaries. From time to time, he would write to one of his brothers in Poland – a few years ago, I met one of that brother's descendants in Warsaw, and discovered to our mutual delight that our rings bore the same crest – but over the years here Gzowski's own sense of Poland dissolved. When the Polish pianist (and later prime minister) Paderewski visited Toronto in the 1890s, the aging Sir Casimir went backstage to greet him, but was so awkward in his mother tongue that he wept in sadness and frustration.

Some day, I will write a book about his extraordinary life, and his impact on our province and our lives.

I'll do it in Rockwood, just across the highway from his barn.

The Country of the Young

Al Purdy

A.Y. Jackson for instance
83 years old
halfway up a mountain
standing in a patch of snow
to paint a picture that says
"Look here
You've never seen this country
it's not the way you thought it was
Look again"
And boozy traders
lost in a dream of money
crews of homesick seamen
moored to a China-vision
hunting the North West Passage
they didn't see it either
The colours I mean
for they're not bright Gauguin
or blazing Vincent
not even Breughel's "Hunters in the Snow"
where you can get lost
and found in five minutes
but the original colour-matrix
that after a giant's heartbeat
lighted the maple forests
in the country south

HERITAGE

A forest clearing of trilliums, official provincial flower, at Sawmill Creek, Mississauga.

(*Right*) A brown doe blends into the flowers and forest foliage in Algonquin Provincial Park, the province's oldest natural sanctuary established in 1893.

(*Below*) The inspiration of many painters, Burleigh Falls is a beauty spot which carries the waters of Lovesick Lake over its flat steps of rock to Stony Lake, the scene of whitewater kayak races each year.

(*Opposite page*) Late afternoon sun glints across snow-covered forest and stream in Cavan township.

(*Opposite page*) A gray mood washes the Scarborough Bluffs as the waters of Lake Ontario slowly erode the face of this unusual cliff formation lying to the east of Toronto.

(*Left*) Minutes from downtown Toronto, the Islands are a parkland complex of lagoons, inlets and beaches. A popular playground, the three islands also offer a boardwalk, restaurants, amusement rides and boating. Once a peninsula, they were severed from the mainland during a major storm in 1858. The view here is of Centre Island.

(*Below*) Winter on the Credit River, near Forks of the Credit, west of Toronto.

(*Below*) A summer day in Pinery Provincial Park near Grand Bend, on Lake Huron, one of the major resorts on the lake.

(*Bottom*) Autumn colours along Medway Creek, near London.

(*Right*) Point Pelee National Park is a 4000-acre wilderness and marshland sanctuary for some 330 varieties of birds. In the path of two major bird migratory flyways, it is also Canada's most southerly mainland point.

(*Opposite page*) Part of the off-shore Georgian Bay Islands National Park, this curious rock-worn chimney formation resembles a huge flower pot, one of many giving Flower Pot Island its name.

(*Left*) Over the rapids during the peak of autumn splendour on the Oxtongue River in Muskoka. The area has been a summer cottage playground since the 19th century.

(*Below*) A deep-blue Lake Huron lies off the Bruce Trail, a major hiking trail along the Bruce Peninsula to Tobermory.

(*Right*) A moose emerges from feeding in a marsh in Algonquin Provincial Park.

(*Below*) A weathered pine tree stands on a rocky inlet in Go Home Bay, typical terrain along Georgian Bay painted by the famous Group of Seven.

(*Opposite page*) Fall gold in Algonquin Provincial Park, near the east entrance to the park.

(*Overleaf*) North of Lake Superior: the dramatic Ouimet Canyon looking west to Lake Nipigon.

(*Right*) Great Horned Owls nesting in February in
the Mississauga area near Toronto. This nocturnal

(*Opposite page*) A stand of birch trees in Emily Provincial Park, north-east of Peterborough.

(*Left*) A cold January day on Batchawana Bay, north of Sault Ste. Marie on Lake Superior. The voyageurs used to pass through this bay on their way north trading for furs.

(*Below*) A beautiful day along an Agawa Bay beach in the rugged Lake Superior Provincial Park, for centuries a plentiful hunting ground of the northern Indians.

(*Below*) An animal skull and antlers adorn the Medicine Man's gate to a three-hundred-year-old Huron Indian village, recently reconstructed near Midland.

(*Opposite page top*) A typical canoe used by the intrepid voyageurs along the Mattawa River in their legendary fur trading with the Indians of the northern interior.

(*Opposite page below*) In 1639 French Jesuits built a fortified mission among the Hurons near present-day Midland. The mission prospered for ten years until the Iroquois to the south, resentful of the French-Huron alliance, and the lucrative fur trade, attacked the outpost and tortured to death Pères Brébeuf and Lalemant.

(*Overleaf*) Red-jacketed cadets drill at Old Fort Henry, Kingston. Once one of Canada's mightiest forts, it was built during the War of 1812 with the United States as a bulwark against an invasion that never came, and is now preserved as an authentic record of 19th century military life.

OBSERVATIONS

Small Town Ontario

Don Harron

Although I am city-born and have never lived in a small town for more than a few weeks at a time, when I escape from my city I retreat to the out-and-out countryside, avoiding suburbs and everything else in between. I must be one of the few Torontonians of my circle of acquaintances who still resides in his home town . . . a community of more than two million. Everyone I run into these days seems to have come here from some small town, and they all maintain fervently that they are heartily glad they left it. On the other hand, those same small towns seem to be filling up with city-born refugees who seem just as grateful to escape from their sordid urban roots.

My first encounter with Ontario small towns in the aggregate was during the summer of 1943 when I worked as a clerk temporarily for the Department of Education. It was my job to ferry high school exam papers from every community in Ontario into the waiting arms of examiners. In this way I got to know the names of every small community from Ardbeg to Zephyr, Drumbo to Vankleek Hill, Consecon to Swastika. But they remained nothing more than words on paper until the fall when I joined the R.C.A.F. I became a bomb-aimer trainee, poring over maps of Ontario and greeting those same places as old familiar friends. The following spring I was able to view most of them from a height of five thousand feet through the cross-hairs of a Norden bombsight.

But my fascination with Ontario place names started even earlier. Between Greenbank and Blackwater are two small places very special to me, Saintfield and Wick. I have relations in both places, and spent vacations in the former locale and six months in 1942 as a hired man near the latter location. I was well fed, and considering my skills, well paid at twenty dollars a month. I was not at all unhappy on the farm, but I needed a place to spend all that money.

It is said that civilization began when people stopped hunting and, gathering, started planting, sitting down together for meals at regular hours. This gave birth to leisure on a full stomach, idle conversation, and eventually abstract and civilizing ideas. Not on my farm. Nothing much beyond pass the butter and the price of canners and cutters and the inner workings of the beef ring. So I ambled down the road after evening chores to the village of Wick. Village? It was a general store, a gas pump, a Presbyterian church and a dog asleep under a tree. But it was possible to buy a Crispy Crunch and a Stone Ginger Beer and exchange civilities with people you knew slightly, and more important, people you didn't know. In this atmosphere I found civilized relations, starting with a discussion of the weather to "Where you from?" and "Whadda yuh think?"

I've noticed this same phenomenon in most small towns I've been in

(*Left*) A 19th century Georgian-style house in Merrickville.

since, a compulsion to reach out to your fellow human. This doesn't happen much in cities where an element of distrust predominates. Cities encourage anonymity. The chief defect of small towns, according to the emigrés who have fled, is that everyone knows your business. Small towns seem to possess their own civilian security service, where they burn up the telephone wires rather than a neighbouring barn. Some might say this is merely an Ontario version of the Moral Majority, encouraging conformity by fear. Oddball individuals do tend to gravitate toward cities, where some of them become our more sensitive artists.

But there is something to be said for the small town as the repository of decency in this late twentieth-century world of ours. Between the decadent sybarites of the cities, and the who-knows-what furtive grapplings going on in or behind the barns of our rural areas, perhaps the small towns of Ontario represent the Middle Way, a path of sanity in a turgid universe.

400: Coming Home

Dennis Lee

You are still on the highway and the great light of
noon comes over the asphalt, the gravelled
shoulders. You are on the highway, there is a kind of
laughter, the cars pound
south. Over your shoulder the scrub-grass, the fences,
the fields wait patiently as though someone
believed in them. The light has laid it
upon them. One
crow scrawks. The edges
take care of themselves, there is
no strain, you can almost hear it, you
inhabit it.

Back in the city many things you lived for
are coming apart.
Transistor rock still fills
back yards, in the parks young men do things to
hondas; there will be
heat lightning, beer on the porches, goings on.
That is not it.

And you are still on the highway. There are no
houses, no farms. Across the median, past the swish and thud of the
northbound cars, beyond the opposite
fences, the fields, the
climbing escarpment, solitary in the
bright eye of the sun the
birches dance, and they
dance. They have
their reasons. You do not know
anything.
Cicadas call now, in the darkening swollen air there is dust
in your nostrils; a
kind of laughter; you are still on the highway.

The Country North of Kingston

Matt Cohen

The country North of Kingston is a civilization with its own laws. The first and most important is that dry must be surrounded by wet, and so the land is seamed by a dense network of streams that join the thousands of swamps and beaverponds, then gather together into rivers and feed the lakes that chain their way from Kingston to Ottawa. Where land and water meet each other, clumps of cedar and pine can be found. On the hills mounting away from lakes and rivers, grow sugar maple and birch. Oak is reserved for the high sandy soil, places that have been scoured by glaciers and worn away by millions of years of weather.

The second law is that land which is cleared must be encircled by trees. True, there are a few fields without their border of elm and maple, but they are the exceptions that prove the rule. The first fields, for example, were the low-lying grassy meadows. Nature had bordered them with trees, but farmers added split-rail fences to keep the cattle in their place. In those fields, too, the first wells were dug. Shallow stone-lined cylinders bored into the wet earth, they can still be seen covered by anything from old car hoods to carefully constructed cement caps.

Harder to make but longer lasting were the fields that had to be cleared. In those places pine grew up so straight and strong that it made masts for ship-yards all over the British Empire. Now those same fields loyally sprout corn or wheat for whoever ploughs and sows them.

It took a hundred years to strip away the forest. Now the trees are coming back, but the original forest can only be imagined, a mysterious mosquito-infested garden of Eden, filled with birds, deer, animals for whom even the names have been forgotten.

The third law has to do with rocks. They are everywhere and of every conceivable type. Black rocks furred with bits of mica glass, yellow sulphurous rock, slabs and seams of pink sparkling granite, gravel pits, limestone quarries and limestone houses, round fieldstones that sprout like gigantic pale eggs from the fields and have been piled into fences and cairns by generations of farmers, fists of prehistoric rock jutting out from anywhere like an unintentional cough. There are so many rocks in the soil North of Kingston that every second car is filled with geologists, tapping at them with their hammers the way a doctor taps at the ribs of a chronically ill patient.

Above the water, the land and the trees is the sky. In the middle of winter the northern lights rise in great glowing shafts. From that beginning the sky can turn itself into almost any colour or shape, and if there are laws that govern the sky, they are still unknown.

Going to the Lake

Alice Munro

We start out once a summer, on a Sunday morning, probably in July, on Highway 86, which we leave at Lucknow, or Whitechurch, or even at Zetland. We zigzag south-west, to Goderich, over the back roads, "keeping the car out of traffic." The jolting it gets on these roads is apparently less damaging to its constitution than the reckless, competitive company of its own kind.

St Augustine. Dungannon. A village called Nile on the map, but always referred to as "the Nile." Places later easily accessible, which seem buried then, in the deep country of hills not cut up for gravel, swamps not drained, narrow dirt roads and one-lane iron bridges. Trees arch across the road and sometimes scrape the car.

The day is always hot, hot enough to make the backs of your legs slick with sweat, to make you long for a drink from a farmhouse pump. There will be dust on the roadside leaves and on the tough plantains that still grow in some places between the wheel-tracks, and a jellifying heat shimmer over the fields that makes the air look as if you could scoop it up with a spoon. Then the look of the sky, to the west, seems to change, to contain a gradual promise of the Lake. Can we really see a difference? Do we imagine it? The subject will come up for discussion — unless my mother is feeling sick, or my father too worried, or we three in the back seat have been put under a disheartening rule of silence, due to a fight. Even then, we cry out, when we top a certain hill, from which you can see — at last, expectedly, and yet amazingly — the Lake. No piddling pond in the rocks and pines but a grand freshwater sea, with a foreign country invisible on the other side. There all the time — unchanging. Bountiful Lake Huron that spreads a blessing on the day. Behind the farms and fences and swamp and bush and roads and highways and brick towns — there all the time.

The sense of the horizon does fade, though, down in Goderich, under the swell of expectation, the accumulating anxieties of pleasure-seekers. Where will we park, when will we eat, remember never to go out past the floats, what are you to do if you get lost? Ahead we hear the shrieks of children on the big slide and the little slide (wet bottoms streaking down the hot metal), the shouts of swimmers and howls of non-swimmers, those terrified children held flat on the water by resolute parents. Boys are jumping and diving and belly-flopping off the pier, and some ladies are lifted squealing on the waves, the skirts of their bathing-suits afloat.

In the park above the beach, in the shade, other ladies are forever laying out and clearing up food, wearing their Sunday dresses. There are old people, country people, lots of people, at this time, who have only work clothes and good clothes. In their good clothes, they picnic at the Lake. The men, in blue serge suits, stand at the edge of the sand, smoking, looking out at the far blue ribbon of water that lightens and brightens as the sun falls from noon. Inlanders, not yet trusting themselves to lakeside enjoyments, except for tobacco, and contemplation. Their faces are brown up to the crease of the caps they don't wear today.

I skid past them, and all the provident wives and the bawling babies under nets — eager to separate, get as lost as I can, plunge alone in the crowded trough of risky pleasures.

Steel City

Sylvia Fraser

I don't know whether there are many streets left in Hamilton where people sit on the front porch with their knitting and newspapers, and the kids on the steps, waiting for things to happen. That's the way it was on our street during The War, and even for a little bit after. Time of day was defined by the breadman, the milkman, the postman, the noon and five o'clock whistles, the newsboy and the street-lights. Days of the week were defined by the iceman, the fruitman, the junkman, the garbageman and *The Star Weekly* carrier, but never, never by the beer truck. Not on *our* street. We were working-class people of careful refinement. A what-will-the-neighbours-think street where women, who had known each other twenty years, called each other Mrs. as they hung the clothes, wore hats to go uptown, and almost-runless stockings for the drugstore.

Of course, for those first six or seven years of life, it didn't much matter whether you were growing up in Hamilton or Moose Jaw. You were expanding like a carrot, by throwing out concentric rings. The universe was defined by a house, then a yard, then a block, then half a dozen of them containing a few small miracles – a magnolia tree that exploded each spring, two chestnut trees and sundry fruit trees, all on someone else's property, and spelling out their seasonal temptations, a vacant lot and a cornerstore, where you were sent, *no loitering, please!* for that missing cake ingredient, with a five-cent popsicle tacked on for good behaviour. The enemy were burrs, bees, dog poop and certain neighbours, Though we didn't have a Witch on our block, we did have a Crabby Lady, a Nosy Lady and a woman who scandalized the rest by wearing men's trousers and collecting steamy horseballs off the road.

Most especially we had our Mountain – at least until that astonishing day when we discovered our cliff of greenery and shale was merely an escarpment! It was never a pretty place but it was a place of privacy and mystery, dark, dense, tangled, slimy and reptilian. A place where lovers could be startled in bushes, where people wrote dirty things on drainage tunnel walls, threw out old bedsprings and, on occasion, dead bodies. That Mountain – a road, a fence and several railway tracks away – recorded your growth as clearly as the family yardstick. You were forbidden to go near it, then only up to the first highway, then – at last! – to the summit, but only with special permission.

When you had mastered the Mountain, you sent out spurlines by rollerskate, by tricycle, then two-wheeler, to discover the peculiarities of your own city.

Hamilton was geographically simple. To the north was The Lake. Uptown was where first-run moviehouses, like the Palace and the Capitol, cost twice as much for half as much as your local theatre, and where the highest building, at sixteen storeys, was Pigott Construction. The coldest and most boring walk was The Market (touted in guide books as a civic wonder) where your father tramped up and down pricing turnips.

Holding all this together was the Beltline streetcar. Rumour had it that buses sometimes, somewhere, ran north and south, but in a dozen years of slogging three miles across town to church, twice on Sunday, I swear I never saw one. It was equidistant travelling east or west by Beltline, and it took about the same time to walk it. Whether to save the car-fare, and get caught halfway in the rain! Whether to go with a friend one way, or to go with another friend the other way! Then the grinding of metal wheels, the smell of wet fur and old galoshes, with mothballs designating a change of season. Lurch, grind, clang-clang, *zzzt*, while you hung by a leather strap, rolling with the skill of a drunken sailor. Only one lure weighted my decision to take the more crowded Uptown route: the chance to stare, for a split-second, down a black side-street to see – all incandescent white-and-gold lightbulbs – my favourite electric sign, spelling out in a pulsating vertical: CUTRATE SHOES. Technological magic pre-*Star Wars*!

I'm not a nostalgia buff. I can't say whether these things were better, or worse. Only that they were.

Great Lake Ships

Gordon Sinclair

Citizens of my generation will remember when Toronto was home port to twelve passenger liners on regular schedule, and one tramp for occasional picnic runs.

Macassa, *Mojeska* and *Turbinia* were all on the Toronto to Hamilton run before there was a mile of paved road in all North America. When such a paved road was built, it was Ontario Number 2 – Toronto to Oakville. It was built on red clay in record time.

There was a park near Dundurn Castle and a little tramp on her Sunday School runs sometimes brought the Hamilton fleet to four. *Turbinia*, fastest of the lot, was secreted away to some mysterious duty during the 1914 to 1918 war. *Macassa* was refitted as a cattle boat, running steers from Manitoulin Island to Owen Sound. She was sunk in an October gale with loss of two-legged and four-legged passengers and I covered the inquest.

The four big C's of the Niagara run, *Chicora*, *Corona*, *Chippewa* and *Cayuga* made daily runs and in August became the most fragrant ships in the world because they were loaded to the safety line by fresh picked peaches.

There were no roads for trucks then; railway box cars were too expensive, so the ships moved tons of peaches when they were truly ripe. None of our modern picking of green fruit and hoping it will semi-ripen before going bad. The Toronto market got tree-ripened and juicy fruit.

Cayuga was the fastest and most durable of those ships. There were several tries at keeping her in service, but the coming of good roads, cheap cars and eighteen-cent gasoline killed that.

The *Dalhousie City* and *Northumberland* took a different course to Niagara, calling at Port Dalhousie rather than Niagara-on-the-Lake so they missed much of the peach trade. Because of crop variation they picked up most of the grape harvest instead. Ontario wine in those days was of inferior quality and most of the juice was used in jelly jam or as an unfermented beverage.

By way of these Niagara ships you could go to Cleveland, Detroit or the Soo and you could steam Toronto to Montreal, entirely by water.

The paddle wheelers, *Toronto* and *Kingston*, took the overnight voyage to Kingston. You could sleep in a stateroom or in the public lounge, and at Kingston passengers switched to the *Rapids King*, *Rapids Queen* or *Rapids Prince* which provided one of the most spectacular steamship voyages through the Thousand Islands and the white waters of the Lachine Rapids to Montreal.

If even this was not enough for the inland mariner from Toronto, passengers could board the *Saguenay* for a scenic cruise on the river from which she took her name and eventually dock beneath the tower of the Chateau Frontenac at Quebec.

There were occasional groundings on the rapids steamers and before the St. Lawrence Seaway was opened, ships sometimes had to sit it out for days until they got extra gushes of water or propeller repairs.

I took one freebie voyage on the *Kingston* and *Rapids Prince* because my uncle was one of the cooks and he made sure I was looked after. I remember finding a wallet in one of the staterooms and when it was returned to its owner, he gave me the unheard of tip of five American dollars.

The *Huronic* and *Noronic*, which were bigger than any vessel in the Toronto fleet, occasionally stopped in Toronto and on one of those occasions, the *Noronic* caught fire, resulting in Toronto's worst marine disaster.

Of all those ships, *Chippewa* was most unusual because of the walking-beam style of mechanism and the sleekest, with speed to spare, was *Turbinia*.

In a modern race, car and ship, downtown Toronto to downtown Hamilton, my bet would be on *Turbinia*, first on the Great Lakes with a turbine engine.

Mariposa

Stephen Leacock

I don't know whether you know Mariposa. If not, it is of no consequence, for if you know Canada at all, you are probably well acquainted with a dozen towns just like it.

There it lies in the sunlight, sloping up from the little lake that spreads out at the foot of the hillside on which the town is built. There is a wharf beside the lake, and lying alongside of it a steamer that is tied to the wharf with two ropes of about the same size as they use on the *Lusitania*. The steamer goes nowhere in particular, for the lake is land-locked and there is no navigation for the *Mariposa Belle* except to "run trips" on the first of July and the Queen's Birthday, and to take excursions of the Knights of Pythias and the Sons of Temperance to and from the Local Option Townships.

In point of geography the lake is called Lake Wissanotti and the river running out of it the Ossawippi just as the main street of Mariposa is called Missinaba Street and the county Missinaba County. But these names do not really matter. Nobody uses them. People simply speak of the "lake" and the "river" and the "main street," much in the same way as they always call the Continental Hotel, "Pete Robinson's" and the Pharmaceutical Hall, "Eliot's Drug Store." But I suppose this is just the same in every one else's town as in mine, so I need lay no stress on it.

The town, I say, has one broad street that runs up from the lake, commonly called the Main Street. There is no doubt about its width. When Mariposa was laid out there was none of that shortsightedness which is seen in the cramped dimensions of Wall Street and Piccadilly. Missinaba Street is so wide that if you were to roll Jeff Thorpe's barber shop over on its face it wouldn't reach halfway across. Up and down the Main Street are telegraph poles of cedar of colossal thickness, standing at a variety of angles and carrying rather more wires than are commonly seen at a transatlantic cable station.

. . . Not that the little town is always gay or always bright in the sunshine. There never was such a place for changing its character with the season. Dark enough and dull it seems of a winter night, the wooden sidewalks creaking with the frost, and the lights burning dim behind the shop windows. In olden times the lights were coal oil lamps; now, of course, they are, or are supposed to be, electricity – brought from the power house on the lower Ossawippi nineteen miles away. But, somehow, though it starts off as electricity from the Ossawippi rapids, by the time it gets to Mariposa and filters into the little bulbs behind the frosty windows of the shops, it has turned into coal oil again, as yellow and bleared as ever.

After the winter, the snow melts and the ice goes out of the lake, the sun shines high and the shanty-men come down from the lumber woods and lie round drunk on the sidewalk outside of Smith's hotel – and that's spring time. Mariposa is then a fierce, dangerous lumber town, calculated to terrorize the soul of a newcomer who does not understand that this also is only an appearance and that presently the rough-looking shanty-men will change their clothes and turn back again into farmers.

Then the sun shines warmer and the maple trees come out and Lawyer Macartney puts on his tennis trousers, and that's summer time. The little town changes to a sort of summer resort. There are visitors up from the city. Every one of the seven cottages along the lake is full. The *Mariposa Belle* churns the waters of the Wissanotti into foam as she sails out from the wharf, in a cloud of flags, the band playing and the daughters and sisters of the Knights of Pythias dancing gaily on the deck.

That changes too. The days shorten. The visitors disappear. The goldenrod beside the meadow droops and withers on its stem. The maples blaze in glory and die. The evening closes dark and chill, and in the gloom of the main corner of Mariposa the Salvation Army around a naphtha lamp lift up the confession of their sins – and that is autumn. Thus the year runs its round, moving and changing in Mariposa, much as it does in other places.

COMMUNITY

A late afternoon hockey game on a frozen pond
near Oakville.

(*Left*) The Peace Tower in Ottawa, framed by autumn's colours, stands guard over the seat of Canada's government. Three Gothic stone buildings roofed with green copper are crowned by the 89-metre tower with a carillon of 53 bells. When Parliament is in session, a white light burns on top of the tower. Ottawa's symbolic location on a hill overlooking the border between Ontario and Quebec, prompted Queen Victoria to proclaim it the capital city in 1857.

(*Below*) Built in the late 1800s, the Provincial Parliament Building is an impressive Victorian edifice of pink sandstone and granite set amongst the shady trees of Queen's Park. The seat of government for the province of Ontario, it contains the Legislative Chamber.

(*Bottom*) The House of Commons in Ottawa, Canada's political core; this is where the nation's business is conducted by elected members from across the country.

(*Opposite page*) The sun shines on the silvery towers of St. Demetrius Ukrainian Orthodox Church in Long Branch, Etobicoke.

(*Left*) Rows of grave markers stand beside an old turn-of-the-century white clapboard church near Nipigon off the Trans-Canada Highway.

(*Below*) The main aisle of St. Paul's, Her Majesty's Chapel of the Mohawks in Brantford, looking towards the altar. Over the altar are the Apostles' Creed, the Ten Commandments and the Lord's Prayer, in the Mohawk language. The famous Six Nations' Chief Joseph Brant is buried here. (*See also page 44*).

(*Opposite page*) A quiet moment at sunset in Toronto's High Park.

(*Left*) Unique modern architecture distinguishes the Brampton County Court House.

(*Below left*) Toronto's finest confer before the beginning of a parade at Varsity Stadium.

(*Below right*) A statue of a Canadian soldier from the First World War stands guard in Peterborough to the memory of those who did not return.

(*Right*) Wawa means "wild goose" in Ojibway. During migration thousands of geese stop over on beautiful Lake Wawa.

(*Below*) Houses in Timmins, once the largest producer of gold in the West. It now boasts the richest silver-zinc mine in the world.

(*Bottom*) Sudbury lies in a huge basin formed by the impact of a giant meteorite about 1700 million years ago. It has made the area rich in gold, platinum, copper, iron, cobalt and nickel.

(*Opposite page*) Situated at the mouth of the Nipigon River, the town of Nipigon was the first white settlement on the north shore of Lake Superior.

(*Opposite page top*) Waiting for the early-morning train going west in Cobourg railway station.

(*Opposite page bottom*) The Algoma Central train stops at the convenience of some local inhabitants and visiting hunters.

(*Left*) Mennonite women enjoy themselves at a festival near Kitchener-Waterloo. A strict Christian sect, they were persecuted in Europe for their pacifist beliefs and came to America. Many retain their simple life and close-knit community to this day.

(*Below*) Mennonites come from all over Waterloo County in their unique horse and buggies to meeting houses such as this one near Heidelberg.

(*Opposite page*) An Ojibway Indian thunders through a colourful dance at the annual Wikwemikong Indian Pow Wow on Manitoulin Island. Manitoulin is the world's largest freshwater island; it has always held special significance for the Indians as a spiritual homeland.

(*Left*) Two Cree Indian girls ride through the Reserve on Moose Factory Island across the river from Moosonee.

(*Below*) Indian children gather to welcome travellers at the Moosonee railway station.

(*Bottom*) An Indian woman cooks bannock bread in her teepee on Moose Factory Island.

(*Right*) Held on Centre Island in Toronto, the giant annual West Indian Festival of Caribana infects the whole downtown core with its exuberance in a burst of music, dancing and exotic costumes.

(*Below*) The Caribana parade joyfully explodes through the streets of Toronto in a panoply of colour and wildly-costumed participants.

(*Bottom*) A happy steel band drummer keeps the beat going at Caribana.

(*Below*) The boys of summer ham it up after a baseball game in Toronto's High Park.

(*Bottom*) Amid the mews, shops and outdoor cafés of Toronto's Yorkville, people take it easy in the afternoon sun.

(*Opposite page*) Wrapped in a gorgeous pink silk sari, a young girl watches an East Indian festival at Toronto's City Hall.

(*Opposite page*) When the Italian soccer team won the World Cup in the summer of 1982, the Italian community in Toronto, the world's largest outside of Italy, burst at the seams with pride, enthusiasm and sheer fun in a week-long non-stop party of green, white and red flags.

(*Below left*) A woman does her daily shopping at one of many outdoor food stalls in the narrow streets of the old Toronto neighbourhood market of Kensington, a bustling patchwork of different cultures.

(*Below right*) A colourful Portuguese candy vendor plies his trade in the crowded streets of Kensington.

(*Right*) Dancers from the Polish Dance Ensemble take a break during the Spring Festival in Toronto's High Park.

(*Below*) A sweet but private ode to love is whispered on a secluded bench in High Park.

(*Opposite page*) A happy clown regales the crowds at Toronto's ultra-modern Eaton Centre.

VOICES

Images of Ontario

Jack Ludwig

Ontario is a sum of images, landscapes, skyscapes, waterscapes – and sounds, and action: a Breughel winterscape of skaters on the Rideau Canal, their blades ringing and scraping, the speeders dipping in and out of the measured unhurried pacers, the whirling figure-skaters as careful as bats at avoiding collision; the hotdogs, the beginners, the small children on bobskates all arrayed in dominating reds and contrasting blacks, brilliant yellows, blues, greens that create a moving changing canvas more than seven kilometres long. In mid-winter the banks are an unbroken white lashed and laced by the shadows of leafless trees. Voices carry easily, shouts of encouragement, warning, the cries of the falling and fallen, peals of laughter. Ottawa in summer is leafy green, grassy, a dazzlement of tulips: nothing takes the place of the vanished skaters. Everything slows down to a loll of greenbank lovers halfhidden by thick foliage and bowers of their own devising.

Above Lake Superior, about fifteen hundred kilometres west of Ottawa, Thunder Bay in winter has not only skaters but ski-jumpers, among the best in the world, who soar into a wintry sky tipped forward at an angle calculated to disarm winds and dissuade gravity, land as coolly as civilians stepping off an escalator. The rugged rock that lies for months under hardpacked snow is magical, full of fabulous colours and crystalline variety: I saw a magnificent fireplace locally mined, locally conceived and hewn from a massive chunk of amethyst that ran from a glassy translucence not unlike rock candy to a deep light-enclosing violet fit for ten thousand birthstones. In coldest winter I saw Kakabeka Falls frozen into amethyst-like solidity from which sunwarmed water dripped steadily in a rainbow of refracted colours. Like the better-known and understandably world-famous Horseshoe Falls of Niagara, Kakabeka is transmogrified by winter's borders and margins, bluewhite milky pillars of ice over which running water was caught and held in a downflow like dripping candlewax; ice armour, ice stalactites, ice spears, ice pennywhistles.

Far to the south, at Point Pelee, on Lake Erie, Ontario is another country: if Ontario with its variety and changes were in Europe it would be the equivalent of a dozen countries. Point Pelee is a crisscross of migrating birdpaths: in spring, flock upon flock moving north; in fall, flocks enlarged by summer's nesting flying south. Thousands of birds arrive and stay. In spring, redwing blackbirds swing on windswayed reeds shrilling their squatter's rights, purple martins swoop over marshwater and back to the cover of surrounding trees, the air percussive with hidden bittern in taller reeds stiff as bamboo. In the midst of these bird days the smelt begin their run, awaited and attended by huge families – great-grandparents, grandparents, fishing fathers, nursing mothers in

(*Left*) Rocky terrain in Ontario's north country.

hipwaders who put down a child and rush in to drag a net corner and dump a heap of writhing slithery small fish onto a plastic sheet. People are lined up for miles in night darkness lit by lanterns and small bonfires, spring's carouse, singing, feasting, jigging, and hard commercial packing of smelts in white pails and barrels.

And. And. And. Spring, summer, autumn, winter.

The images of Ontario are numberless.

The Path of Life

Basil Johnston

Our ancestors taught us – and the Midewewin teaches us – that there is a Land of Souls. In that land there is no sickness, no hunger, no sorrow, no anger, and no envy. It is a Land of Peace inhabited by men and women of peace. For them there is plenty and comfort and joy.

Our ancestors tell us that only men and women of peace may enter there. Others will suffer hardship and misfortune and sickness in this life. Or they will be caught in the river that divides the Land of the Living from the Land of Souls.

The Midewewin tells us that we must lead good lives – following the Path of Life. The Path of Life will give us good fortune, good health, and peace of heart in this world; and bring us admission into the Land of Souls.

And the Midewewin tells us what the Path of Life is.

We must honour Kitche Manitou and thank him for life – for the winds, the sun, the waters, and the land we live on.

We must honour our elders – for they are the recipients of a great gift of long life from Kitche Manitou. If they are slow and feeble and sometimes infirm, we must feed them, help them, listen to them, and be patient. That is also our destiny. Someday we, too, will be old.

We must honour our elder brothers – the wolf and the bear, the eagle and the robin, the snake and the turtle, the butterfly and the snail, the whitefish and the trout. We must honour the rose and the corn. On them we depend for food and clothing. Treat them well, so that when you want them they will allow you to take them. You will never need. They will look after you.

We must honour women – our grandmothers and mothers, our wives and our sisters, and all the others. Treat your wife with kindness. She is your companion and friend on the Path of Life. Look after her and she will look after you. Comfort her, cheer her, speak well of her and all her sisters.

We must keep our promises and uphold our pledges. If we undertake to do something for another, we must fulfil our word by deed – otherwise we are false. If we receive a vision we must live out the vision – otherwise we are untrue. Without truth to self and to others there is no trust.

We are to be kind to everyone. Children listening to their parents: that is kindness. Parents teaching their children: that is kindness. A hunter giving meat to the elderly or to the widowed: that is kindness. A medicine man or woman healing the sick: that is kindness. A woman feeding a stranger: that is kindness. A man sheltering a stranger: that is kindness. Do something for your people. Use your gifts and your dreams for good.

We are to be peaceful. Dark dreams beget more dark dreams, and

90

cause clouded, troubled thoughts. Twisted thoughts stir up violent passions; boiling passions give rise to burning words; and fiery speech breeds hurts and bad deeds. Seek good dreams. Temper your thoughts, your passions, your words, and your deeds. All this is hard to achieve. But we must strive for peace of heart in this life and peace of soul in the next.

Lastly, we are to be moderate in our dreams, thoughts, words, and deeds. We are never to indulge too much in one thing at the expense of another. Do not play too much; do not sleep too long. Do not eat too much; do not talk too often. Listen and watch. Someday you will be wise.

Aux origines de l'Ontario: une province séparée et dépendante du Québec

Fernand Ouellet

Depuis des générations, les Ontariens aiment à se représenter leur province comme le foyer principal et permanent depuis presque toujours de diffusion du sentiment national à l'échelle du pays. Leur idée d'une nation dont le destin se serait forgé un peu moins à partir de la contribution de ses composantes régionales qu'à partir du rôle dominant d'une communauté particulière, la leur, a été largement épousée par les historiens anglophones qui ont élaboré les grands schémas interprétatifs du passé canadien. Bien qu'ils admettent sans trop de peine le concept d'une nation bi-culturelle, façonnée en partie par les francophones, et qu'ils relient l'origine de leur province aux réclamations spécifiques des *Loyalistes*, ces historiens ont néanmoins tendance à rechercher les racines du Haut-Canada naissant dans un passé plus lointain et à lui attribuer dès le jour de sa fondation une sorte de pré-science de sa mission en tant que centre fédérateur du pays dans son ensemble.

Même si cette reconstruction du passé avait un sens par rapport à un projet national, le fait demeure que le territoire ontarien, bien que sillonné en toutes directions depuis toujours par les Indiens et, depuis le XVIIième siècle, par les marchands de pelleteries, les coureurs des bois et les engagés pour la traite, ne constituait avant 1791 qu'une partie non identifiée d'un espace économique, politique et culturel plus vaste qui, depuis Champlain, s'étendait du Golfe St-Laurent au Pacifique et dont le centre se trouvait à Québec et à Montréal. La division du Québec en deux provinces distinctes pour répondre aux voeux de certains groupes loyalistes ne signifiait cependant pas une rupture complète des liens avec le passé. La séparation politique, celle qui était la plus manifeste et qui parût tellement arbitraire à ceux qui, au Québec, participaient toujours en grand nombre au commerce des pelleteries, fut loin d'être totale puisque le parlement du Bas-Canada eut le droit exclusif d'imposer des taxes sur les produits importés de la haute mer à Québec, peu importe leur destination, et, cela, sans l'avis et la participation des Hauts-Canadiens eux-mêmes. Ce ne fut qu'à la suite de négociations fort ardues entre les représentants des deux colonies que les règles du partage de ces revenus, toujours plus ou moins équitables pour le partenaire le plus faible, furent revisées par la suite. Car, le Haut-Canada n'avait pas de débouché direct sur la mer et bien des décisions parmi les plus importantes pour son développement étaient prises soit à Montréal soit à Québec. Pour l'importation des produits nécessaires à sa population, pour l'expédition de ses surplus de production, pour l'amélioration des communications et pour l'obtention de crédit, la nouvelle colonie dépendait, d'une façon ou d'une autre, plus que de raison de la colonie voisine. Comme autrefois et pour longtemps encore, Montréal assuma la fonction de métropole commerciale et financière de cette partie du pays.

Frustrés, des Hauts-Canadiens allèrent même jusqu'à réclamer vers 1829 l'annexion de Montréal à leur province. Nombreux furent ceux qui eurent le sentiment que leur province, encore peu développée, n'était guère plus qu'une colonie du Bas-Canada et ils souhaitèrent échapper à cette emprise. Bien loin d'appuyer en majorité les projets d'union des Canadas, particulièrement au moment des crises de 1810 et de 1822, les Hauts-Canadiens gardèrent leurs distances à l'égard des visées des marchands anglophones de Québec et de Montréal. Même en 1840, lorsque l'union des Canadas fut sur le point d'être imposée et que, sur les plans économique et démographique, leur province parût désormais assurée d'une suprématie en ces domaines, ils étaient encore pour la plupart tellement imbus du sentiment de leur faiblesse qu'au lieu de réclamer la représentation selon la population, ils acceptèrent plus que volontiers un système qui, dans l'assemblée législative du Canada-uni leur garantissait le même nombre de députés qu'à l'autre Canada. Il fallut encore une bonne décennie avant qu'ils ne commencent à entrevoir les contours de leur rôle dominant dans un Canada dont les frontières, débordant celles du Canada central, inclueraient éventuellement les Maritimes et les territoires de l'ouest.

Some Odd Mammals

Graeme Gibson

Shuffling purposefully, as if we weren't there, the porcupine reached the bole of a pine tree and had begun to climb by the time he returned with an axe from our ice house. Heavy-bodied and short-legged, it paused about three feet from the ground until Donald caught it a terrible blow that knocked it squealing into the underbrush beside the path leading to the furthest privy. There were two outhouses at our summer home; one for men and another, which was closer to the house, for women. There was also a small bedroom off the kitchen in case we ever had a maid.

This happened in Muskoka when there were fish in the lake and steamers, with buntings, blasted their whistles by the pier on the mainland. A hard, eccentric man, Donald did odd jobs for summer people, and lived, alone, in an evil-looking cabin by the boathouse next to his parents' beaten garden.

He also painted dire warnings on the pre-Cambrian shield. REPENT OR BE DAMNED FOR HE IS AN ANGRY GOD AND HELL AWAITS YOU. Some insisted he roamed the bush bare-arsed naked, sneaking up on groups of berry pickers, but I never saw that. . . .

He was born after his parents came from England at about the time my grandfather built on the island in the 1890s. His father had been to Oxford. They even say he'd graduated. Moving in his garden with the melancholy precision of a heron, the old man wore suits that were dusty and out of place, as if he'd found them in an attic. I never figured out what he was doing there.

For years, whenever I entered the cubbyhole post office in their house, his ancient wife stared with an air of benign madness, as if she'd never seen me before. Through a partially open door I sometimes saw their parlour filled with books and stuffed furniture, the whole of it smelling of varnish and sunlight.

Wildly beautiful, with the rolling echoes of train whistles tumbling down the lake and back again, Muskoka was a hard place to homestead, a bad place to farm. Even then I tried to see, in those closed faces, some hint of the people who had discovered they were leaving Oxford for these rocks, this unforgiving land. What a falling away, it seemed! And what did they make of their son?

My parents hadn't meant for him to kill the porcupine. They just wanted it gone so it wouldn't eat the rest of the pump handle, but Donald didn't care. Because he couldn't get a clear swing, he golfed it back onto the path where it convulsed, opening and closing like a hand, until he finished the job.

Then he took it away with him in the green canoe, fitted with oars, in which he delivered the mail. It wasn't until years later, in England, that I recognized that easy sculling stroke – at a boat race.

The Algoma Hills

Morley Callaghan

McLaughlin began to talk about the fishing villages and the black flies in the bush that came down to the shore line, till the newspapermen he was playing with objected angrily to his interrupting the game. "I don't know why," McLaughlin said apologetically, "but that guy's got the Algoma shore country on the brain." Peter grinned and lied, "I was up there once when I was a kid." No one doubted him because he had the look in his eyes of a man who was trying to remember half-forgotten, far-away things; it was as though some one had waved a wand in front of him and showed him where the journey might have led. In his pocket he had two railroad maps marking the route to the Algoma Hills, and showing where the lake boats touched the mainland. He had persisted further and found out how far north along the shore the gravel road extended before ending in rock and timber. He had found out that there was an Ojibway Indian reserve far along the shore from the river and the Mission. It was much harder to find out how long the French people had been at the Mission, for no one knew, and no books told about them. He read about the gold mines of the country that had been wildcatted, and the vast iron ore deposits; and without ever having seen it, he could talk glibly about the blue lake teeming with whitefish and lake trout, and of the abundance of pickerel at the river mouths. He had found out all these things like a man who learns about the things he expects to encounter if he should ever have the good fortune to make a long-postponed journey.

. . . It was late in the afternoon when the steamer crossed the wide mouth of the Michipicoten River and passed the yellow sandbar, and the point of black jutting rock. At the dock there was a small shed, a government warehouse and a dirt road leading back through the wooded hills. On a small sandy beach littered with washed-up and sun-baked wood, five round squat Indian women sat huddled together on a log, their black shawls over their shoulders, watching passengers get off the steamer for an hour's walk on the sand. The boat would remain at the dock till supplies were unloaded and then go farther on up the north shore.

. . . That evening at twilight, when Peter was alone, he lay very still, trying to get the feeling of the special quality of the country. The hours were long. A moon rose early. The room – the wall by the bed – was splashed with moonlight. He was aware of the dark, majestic, encroaching hush, and felt uneasy. At this time every night a big bull moose came out to the river a little way down the shore to drink and look out over the water. Peter wanted to have in him some of the strength of the loneliness of the country.

Witness

Timothy Findley

Film is a witness. It speaks in behalf of both past and future. Because of its nature, film distils and concentrates: it freezes and reveals whole segments of time. A recent experience in film-making reveals such a segment of time and, with it, the look and the sound of a part of Ontario society that has been with us since the days of Governor Simcoe and the Reverend John Strachan. This experience was the making of a film called *The Wars*.

Technically, *The Wars* must be called an historical film because it begins in 1914 and ends in 1917. However, in more than one sense, it transcends that period and passes not only forward into the future where we are living now, but backward into the distant past where the values were formed by which the people in *The Wars* lived out their lives. It shows this not only through the voices of its characters, but through the voices of its creators.

Like every film, *The Wars* was created in concert. In the course of each stage of its transformation from book to screenplay to film, a new voice was added: the director's voice, the designer's voice, the voices of the actors and the composer's voice. Each of these voices, in its turn, brought a unique interpretation of the language we speak, of the landscape we live in and of the sounds and images we have invented to define our culture.

The director, Robin Phillips, had been working in the Canadian theatre for ten years – and, before that, in England. What he brought to the film was the confirmation of something we have never quite admitted existed here: a tradition of style and form and love of language. He laid this tradition before us and forced us to examine it. In this way, the making of *The Wars* began with the confidence of knowing it was not emerging from that widely trumpeted "cultural void" we had been taught to believe was our provincial birthright, but from a living culture whose roots are in our own backyard. The designer, Daphne Dare, had the wonderful notion that the past in which this story takes place was still alive in the stones of Ontario's houses and churches, its graveyards and gardens. Consequently, our province has never looked more like itself and less like anywhere else. Every room and every stick of furniture, every piece of hand-painted wallpaper, every painting and every photograph, every lamp and every plate makes up a part of the voice of our collective past. Even the light filtered through the windows is the light we have lived by since our birth in this place.

As for the voices of the actors, they carry the authority of our language as it is, with all its tricks of social pretension and cultural insecurity, on the one hand, and the vitality of its native honesty on the other. Lastly, there is the music. It was Glenn Gould's intention, when he took on this assignment, to bring all the music out of "an Edwardian piano bench" such as might be found in a middle-class Toronto household, circa 1914. His score, therefore, is a musical portrait of Ontario both of the past and of the present. Parlour songs, hymns and marching songs still with us abound on the soundtrack together with the piano pieces that have thwarted generations of adolescents struggling to master the contents of their red-coated R.C.M. exercise books.

There is a choral effect in *The Wars*, both visual and aural: a blending of all the voices through which we speak of who we are. The sombre, upright men and women walking through snow – the families gathered at dining-room tables laden with the harvest of Ontario gardens – the children in their tam-o-shanters, mittens and scarves, sliding on the ice – the dark, Victorian stained-glass windows half-way up the stairs – the railroad cars and the rainy stations we have known, it seems, forever. And the portraits and photographs of our ancestors, fading at the edge of incomprehensible hardships, the harshness and horror of which would ultimately define us all.

Perhaps it takes two hundred years for any people to find its voice. It shouldn't – but, perhaps, it does. We can be grateful, then, that for us the two hundred years is over. We are its witness. And we have the voice to say so.

North of Superior

Earle Birney

Not here the ballad or the human story
the Scylding boaster or the water-troll
not here the mind   only the soundless fugues
of stone and leaf and lake   where but the brutish
ranges   big with haze   confine the keyboard

Barbaric the clangour of boulders   the rhythm of trees
wild where they clutch the pools   and flying with flame
of their yellow sap are the stretching poplars of May
running arpeggios up to the plangent hills

The horseman icecap rowelled the only runes
and snow-wild wind these eochromes upon
the raddled rocks that wear the tarns like eyes
within their saurian skulls   O none alive
or dead has cast Excalibur into
these depths   or if some lost Algonquin wooed
a dream that came and vanished here   the breeze
today shakes blades of light without a meaning.

Unhaunted through the birches' blanching pillars
lopes the mute prospector   through the dead
and leprous-fingered birch that never led
to witches by an Ayrshire kirk nor wist
of Wirral and a Green Knight's trysting

Close march the spruce   and 'fir that weepeth ever'
the wandering wood that holds no den of Error
Silently over the brush they lift their files
and spear forever together the empty sky
Not here the rooted home but only discords

the logger sounds   tarpaper shanty scored
with lath he deeds next year to squirrel and spider
and little wounds upon the rocks the miner
makes and leaves at last to mending snow
The wood returns into its soil   the caribou
are blurring hoofmarks in the scrub   gray wolf
and man make flickers on the long horizon

This world that is no world except to hunted
purblind moose and tonedeaf passing hunter
yet skirls unheard its vast inhuman pibroch
of green on swarthy bog   of ochre rock
and the wine that gleams through the spectral poplar's bark
Not here   with hymn and carol blessed   Titania's
night   nor will this neuter moon in anger
pale for vanished rites or broken bough
For nocturne   hypnosis of lynx and owl
No heart to harden or a god to lose
rain without father   unbegotten dews

See where the unexorcized dragon   Fire
has breathed unwieldy lances from the wilds
for wars already waged   and planted one
charred pine to fly a pennant still   a husk
of golden needles – yet no mute or glorious
Milton finds Azazel here   no Roland
comes to blow defiance by this serpent stream

No sounds of undistinguishable motion
stalk the guilty poet flying   only
silence where the banded logs lie down
to die and provender the luminous young
The swordless rock   the heavenless air   and land
that weeps unwept into an icy main
where but the waters wap and the waves wane

C.P.R. trains 1926/1946

96

ENTERPRISE

Optical fibres are the transmission medium of the
future, offering communication that can at once
relay voice, data and video. In 1978, Bell Canada
began the world's first field trial of a fibre optics
system to serve residence telephones.

(*Opposite page*) Red-hot billets stand ready for shipping to the rolling mill at the Dofasco steel mill in Hamilton.

(*Left*) Miners drill blast holes to extract gold from the rock face in the Campbell Lake Gold Mine in northwestern Ontario.

(*Below left*) The assembly-line at the General Motors of Canada car plant at Oshawa.

(*Below right*) A Consumers' Gas rig on Lake Erie near Port Burwell.

(*Bottom*) Fort Frances is a prosperous paper town on Rainy Lake.

PURSUITS

The Bay Street Game

Alexander Ross

The Toronto Stock Exchange may have moved around the corner to King Street, most of the mining promoters may have fled to Vancouver and, at sidewalk level, you may notice more drugstores and coffee shops than brokerage houses. But Bay Street is still the spiritual and geographical centre of Canadian finance, and its mythology still exerts a powerful influence on the Canadian imagination.

Money may be only a commodity, like soybeans or pork bellies. But in the black and gold and marble skyscrapers that constitute the village that is Bay Street, money, and a continual torrent of information about money, are essences you can almost breathe. You can smell it in the vast reception areas of the big corporate law firms, designed to overawe their clients with oriental tapestries and circular staircases of dark, expensive wood. You can sense it in the neurotic clamour around a hundred circular trading desks, crammed with computer consoles and chittering news tickers, where young, shirtsleeved traders (there are very few old ones) bark into telephones and exchange billions of dollars worth of stocks, bonds, currencies and commodities every day. You can savour it in the top-floor dining-rooms of the great banks, where important corporate clients are entertained at lunch in surroundings that resemble Georgian country houses. And you can witness the almost feral urgency of money, the serum of the street, on the squash courts and rooftop jogging track of the Cambridge Club, an athletic club hidden at the top of an unmarked elevator in the Sheraton-Four Seasons complex, where some of the street's leading shooters come daily to whip their bodies into a state of competitive readiness.

The cacophonous centre of this bazaar is the new trading floor of the Toronto Stock Exchange, not much smaller than a football field and, when the market is running, almost as noisy as Grey Cup Night. In a slow year, the TSE will trade more than twenty-five billion dollars worth of securities, which is more than seventy percent of the entire Canadian total. The place is an electronic zoo. There are hundreds of video monitors, thousands of telephone lines; and most of the thousand-odd floor traders wear electronic pagers which, because of the noise level on the floor, vibrate instead of emitting beeps.

It all started in 1856, when a group of local businessmen erected an imposing domed building on Wellington Street to trade cattle and grain futures. By the early years of this century, mining booms in B.C. and northern Ontario had transformed the street into one of the world capitals of institutionalized chicanery. From the '20s to the '60s, its character was defined mainly by its tribe of sleazy mining promoters, who peddled worthless mining shares across the continent by long-distance telephone. In the 1930s, in a belated wave of reform, more than thirty of Bay

(*Left*) A country road near Mount Forest.

Street's Finest were sent to prison. But the game continued merrily on until 1964, when a particularly egregious manipulation known as the Windfall Scandal forced Bay Street to clean up its act.

Since then, the street has settled down to the sonorities of institutional trading, government bond issues, corporate underwritings and other profitable but colourless pursuits. There hasn't been a truly juicy scandal involving a Bay Street securities firm for years and years. But the larceny in men's souls, that primitive need to best one's fellow-human, is still the salt and savour of the street. The referees may be more vigilant, the customers may have a better chance of getting what they paid for, the players may commit fouls only when they believe the referees aren't watching; but the Bay Street game goes on.

Advocates

Jack Batten

The sixty-three Ontario barristers who gathered on the May evening in 1965 didn't think of the occasion as specifically a celebration of themselves and their profession. But that is what it, in effect, turned out to be, a mutual recognition that their talents as counsel who performed wonders of argument and cross-examination and jury address in the province's courtrooms, placed them on a different – and perhaps loftier – plateau than their brethren at the bar.

The May 1965 meeting marked the founding of The Advocates' Society. It was an organization limited to those Ontario lawyers "whose sole or principal occupation is the practice of advocacy before the law courts," and over the years, as its membership escalated to the one thousand mark by 1983, the Society has launched itself on ambitious programs of education and fellowship. Its members stage semi-annual conferences on the thornier aspects of the art of advocacy. They journey off every second year to share ideas and good times with counsel in foreign jurisdictions, in Ireland and Israel and Australia and California. And they sit over lunches of chops, wine and trifle in Campbell House, the elegant 1822 residence that they restored and relocated as their headquarters across the street from Osgoode Hall in downtown Toronto.

But in a sense the fundamental purpose of the Society is to keep alive the grand tradition of that remarkable breed – the Ontario barrister. The province has always been blessed with colourful and nervy counsel, men like Thomas Cowper Robinette who ranged through the courts in the early years of the twentieth century and whose style was once described in these gaudy terms: "His opening syllables arrested the attention of usually immovable magistrates. Courts hung on his accents. He touched men in their most vulnerable parts. It is not mere rhetoric to say that tears flowed copiously and hearts melted noticeably during his passionate appeals."

And there were others, gifted counsel glorying in a magnificent variety of courtroom battles. The revered W.N. Tilley dominated the civil bar through the middle years of the century, a blunt operator who attacked with the bludgeon, and during the same period, Arthur Slaght reigned as the star of the criminal courts, employing as his principal weapon an eloquence that dazzled.

But it was in the years after the Second World War that Ontario counsel emerged in larger numbers and more sweeping skills. Joe Sedgwick played the role of the mellifluous orator of the courts and Dave

Humphrey came on as the stand-up comedian among criminal defence counsel. Ken Howie and Martin Wunder made their marks as plaintiffs' advocates, winning justice and compensation for clients who had been cruelly injured through others' negligence. Some lawyers developed specialties in narrow and demanding fields, Julian Porter in libel actions, Brian Greenspan in criminal appeals, Ian Scott in labour cases.

Then there was John Josiah Robinette, the son of T.C. Robinette. Of all Ontario counsel, he has been our real-life Perry Mason, a lawyer for the courtroom and a lawyer for the headlines. In his long career, he has defended sixteen accused murderers (only one was convicted), represented both big business and concerned citizens, and argued all of the constitutional cases on behalf of the federal government through the 1970s and '80s. His range has been breathtaking, and it was only natural that in the summer of 1979, The Advocates' Society would plant a tree on the lawn of Campbell House that marked the fiftieth anniversary of Robinette's call to the Ontario bar.

"Among the tall timber at the bar," another splendid counsel, Barry Pepper, said on that occasion, "John J. Robinette has stood out like an oak."

And in thus celebrating Robinette, the barristers were at the same time celebrating their own unique and marvellous kind.

Stars of the Medical Theatre

Donald Jack

Ontario gave to the world Dr. Murray Barr and his work on the cellular determination of sex, James Collip, who was the first to isolate ACTH, William Osler, the most renowned physician since Hippocrates, Frederick Banting, who conquered diabetes, Norman Bethune, who conquered China. And so on. But the province's contribution resides as much in the character of its doctors as in their accomplishments. It is the lives and individual personalities of its people that most truly enrich a region and give it distinction. People like William Dunlop, a giant, carroty-haired Scotsman who arrived in Ontario as a British army surgeon in the War of 1812. He came to open up the patients and stayed to open up the country. He fell in love with the Canadian backwoods, where his riproaring way of life, and his learning, his wild humour, and love of unpretentious people were to make him a legendary figure. As an employee of the Canada Company he used his rackety personality to dominate every sort of company from tavern brawlers to the sluggish toffs of the colonial aristocracy. He could create drama out of disrobing. Once, after a day in the sodden forest, upon joining a woodland party of pompous Canada Company officials, he flung off his clothes and danced naked round the camp fire, singing violently. He was regarded with deep appreciation by the Indians, and with outrage from his boss, the distinguished but utterly circumspect novelist, John Galt. When the Company sent an unpleasant little Cockney named Smith to investigate Dr. Dunlop's affairs as "Warden of the Forest," the good doctor led him into the woods, programming him all the way with frightful tales of man-eating wolves. That night Dunlop slipped into the darkness and proceeded to howl from every point of the compass. Smith was so agitated that he flung himself upon his horse and fled in almost as many directions, until he was swiped out of the saddle by an overhanging branch. That was the last time Smith ever attempted to supervise the doctor, enabling Dunlop to go on enjoying the free life of a Canadian settler, "which is lacking in a more civilized country."

Frequently our early doctors were not only roistering but revolutionary. Like Drs. Duncombe and Rolph, who co-founded the province's first medical school, the Talbot Dispensatory. They had prominent roles in the Mackenzie Rebellion, and were forced to flee for their lives. Duncombe ran to the border disguised as a woman, and even prevailed on a militiaman to help "her" across the Detroit River ice. A century later, Dr. Morton Shulman was still maintaining the Ontario tradition of the doctor as radical when, as chief coroner in Toronto, he refused to hush up various scandals involving the establishment, the medical profession, and the bureaucracy.

Women doctors also contributed to the aggressive tradition, in their case because fighting for their rights was the only way to counter several thousand years of hostility to women in medicine. Round the turn of the century, it took pretty Elizabeth Scott, who commenced her training at the Women's Medical College, Kingston, sixteen years to be accepted by the medical profession. The hostility was still evident forty years later when Marion Hilliard was on her way to becoming the country's foremost obstetrical specialist at the Women's College Hospital.

Toronto's William Beaumont invented many surgical instruments and the principle of the Singer sewing machine; the University of Toronto's Davidson Black discovered Peking Man; and two of the most famous doctors in the world in the 1930s were Ontario country doctors, Dafoe of the North Bay Quintuplets fame, and Mahlon Locke, the miraculous foot doctor of Williamsburg.

We have good reason to be proud of their individualism and enriching personalities, as well as their accomplishments.

A City of Learning

Robertson Davies

Many people think that the purpose of a university is to provide useful knowledge and contribute to the betterment of life, and they are right. Dispute may arise, however, about what is useful. One of the glories of the University of Toronto has been its contribution of insulin to the world. Because of its discovery there in 1922 millions of people have been delivered from certain death. It might be argued, however, that the University's edition of the works of Erasmus, which is now in progress, is as great an achievement in a wholly different realm. One is research: the other is scholarship. Both enrich society, and their existence together in our University makes it a true *universitas*, a body of scholars seeking to preserve, enlarge and teach all knowledge, the immediately applicable and the potentially influential.

The love-hate relationship that exists between a university and its community is rooted in the demand of society that the university earn its place in the lifeboat, so to speak, by pushing ahead the obvious frontiers of knowledge, which are seen as belonging to the world of science, while at the same time the university is expected by society to conserve whatever is of value in the past. The two jobs cannot be done by men of the same sort. The scientist, however unworldly he may seem, is regarded with an awe little short of superstitious, whereas the scholar in the humanities may look to the public like a man who is merely enjoying himself, a condition intolerable in one who has, in our society, become very much a member of the civil service. Preserving the balance between love and hate, and serving the community as only a university can, is a task that demands the uttermost from university administrators.

Upon the whole, the University of Toronto has done very well in this struggle, and its achievement, as the oldest and largest of Ontario's universities, provides example and encouragement to younger institutions. Much of its strength lies in its college system, which gives so many of its graduates a double loyalty, first to the college, which is an academic home, rich in memories and friendships, and second to the Alma Mater – truly the Bounteous Mother – which has added to college life so many things that pertain to a City of Youth, which is also a City of Learning, a City of Pleasure, and a gateway to life, the gifts from which are recognized and enjoyed long after university days are over. If indeed, they are ever over. The loyalty of Toronto's graduates suggests that the link is one that endures for a lifetime.

Discovery and Invention

J. Tuzo Wilson

The list of important Ontario discoveries and inventions is impressive, but all too often their origins have been lost because of lack of Canadian interest or because large companies elsewhere have developed them. And yet, as the record clearly shows, the myriad discoveries made in this province is something we can all be proud of.

The problem of early settlers in Canada was to feed themselves. We have all heard the accomplishments of John McIntosh of Dundas, David Fyfe of Peterborough and Sir Charles Saunders in improving strains of apples and wheat, but who is aware that Thomas Carroll of Toronto developed the first self-propelled combine for Massey-Harris? Other nations had developed most forms of agricultural machinery, but Carroll's machine was the first to mow, thresh, separate, clean and bag grain in one sweep.

In 1892, Thomas Ahearn cooked a gourmet meal at the Windsor Hotel in Ottawa as the first demonstration of the electric stove which he had just invented. Few Canadians realize this or that E. Asselbergs and W.H. Cook also of Ottawa pioneered processes for drying food, while Professor Archibald Huntsman first successfully froze food fast so that it would keep its flavour. Other Toronto doctors invented Pablum.

Transportation is another matter of vital importance to Canada. The Rideau Canal, begun in 1827 before railways had been invented, and its successors the Welland, Trent and Seaway Canals have all been leaders in their time. Among many improvements to rail transportation, no Canadian invention has been more important than the rotary snow-plow on which J.W. Elliott of Toronto obtained the basic patent in 1869, and which was developed into practical use for the Canadian Pacific Railway by Orange Jull and the Leslie brothers, all of Orangeville. The design is now in world-wide use, along with many other Canadian inventions for dealing with snow.

Another Canadian first in transportation was the earliest diesel locomotive built for Canadian National Railways in Kingston and soon copied all over the world. In 1878, Sir Sandford Fleming introduced Standard Time, now in universal use. Street railways became safe and reliable in 1863 when J.J. Wright invented the trolley pole and overhead line.

In communications, Alexander Graham Bell said he first conceived of the telephone and began experiments in Brantford in 1874 and 1875, but the following spring achieved the first transmission in Boston. In August 1876, back in Ontario, he quickly built the first long telephone lines, switchboards and modern receivers which together made telephoning practical.

Among the many Canadian contributions to radio, Ted Rogers of Toronto in 1925 patented the first radio operated by lighting circuits instead of batteries. More recently, the Department of Communications and Canadian companies have produced many of the most significant satellites including the *Alouette* and *Anik* series. And the National Research Council funded, and Spar Aerospace developed, designed and built the successful Space Arm to launch and recover satellites in space. Also in Ontario W.R. Franks invented the first space suit for pilots while others developed most of the de-icing equipment used on aircraft today.

In chemistry, Thomas L. Willson of Woodstock was a prolific inventor, best known for first making acetylene cheaply. In the 1880s it was used for lighting, but since 1903 the oxyacetylene torch has played a key role in metal fabrication.

In 1971, Gerhard Herzberg of Ottawa received the Nobel Prize for life-long work on atomic spectra. And John Polanyi's work in chemical kinetics led to the development of the laser.

In physics, the University of Toronto built the first successful electron-microscope in 1938, and originated the Cobalt-60 bomb for medical use. Atomic Energy of Canada produced the world's most powerful and reliable reactor, while the Canadian National Research Council has developed the most accurate clocks.

In this bicentennial year it is good to record a few of the useful things invented and discovered by the ingenious people of Ontario. We should learn to take a greater pride in our achievements and so derive the profit which we have by our neglect allowed others to do in the past.

Decision City

Peter C. Newman

Toronto is Downtown Canada.

Technopolis-on-the-Humber is a 240-square-mile city-state that spreads its arrogance across the country, dispassionately dispensing money, heroes, culture, alienation, advice and predestiny. If Montreal is a city of heritage and Vancouver a city of style, Toronto is a city of influence.

This is very different from political power, which is carefully husbanded – camouflaged by slogans, smiles and supplications. Unlike the tides of shifting favouritism inside the political courts of Ottawa, the Toronto power structure works on a simple principle: you're in, or you're out. If you're in, you're on top, swinging with the high-rollers who know how to deify the heroes of the hour.

Power in Toronto is constantly on the move, being snared by some, eluding others. Glamour-fields wane. Names disappear from contention. Phones stop ringing. Hardly anyone has time to notice, for instance, that the FOOFS (Fine Old Ontario Families) aren't in charge any more. There's a restaurant in the Massey house on Jarvis Street; hordes of long-haired students from Etobicoke pound through the once-aristocratic Falconer Hall on their way to classes; the Gooderham mansion has become a club;

a developer lives in Lady Eaton's former house on Old Forest Hill Road; no one cares who belongs to the Rosedale Golf Club any more. The Mullocks and the Cawthras are all but forgotten.

It's the technostructure that counts now – the interchangeable lawyers, the accountants, engineers, architects and, most of all, the money-men. They're in perpetual motion, more familiar with flight schedules to Cleveland and Atlanta and the hotels of Buenos Aires than the Manitoba Club or Vancouver's Shaughnessy Heights. They fragment their psyches, constantly trying to stretch their authority, knowing they're only as good as their last deal. "We all need to be within a thousand feet of one another. That's how business gets done," says Michael Koerner, an international investor who works out of one of the Toronto-Dominion towers.

Members of the Toronto Establishment never cease monitoring the state of their own influence. The quickest test is that, no matter who they're phoning, they always get through. (If you're asked to hold, you're slipping; if you're asked to leave your number at the "message centre," forget it.)

It's the only Canadian city in which the local elite almost automatically qualifies for cross-country status. Nearly three-quarters of the certified members of Canada's national Establishment live within the Toronto commutershed.

With its nearly eighty million square feet of office space, Toronto is twice as dominant in relation to its economic hinterland as is New York, which has only fifteen percent of the available U.S. office accommodation. Manhattan is the home address of about one-tenth of *Fortune*'s 500, while Toronto houses fully half of the corporate head offices in similar Canadian listings. Every working day, at least one and a half billion dollars changes hands – ranking Toronto as the world's fifth most significant financial centre.

Even though Canada is becoming politically more decentralized, economically it's being drawn ever more tightly within Toronto's orbit. No other place can marshall the necessary facilities rapidly enough. Whether you're building a shopping centre in Prince George, financing a motel in Brandon, throwing a pipeline across the Rockies, refinancing a lollipop factory at La Tuque or fashioning yourself a dandy offshore tax haven in the Cayman Islands, Toronto is the only place with the expertise and money that can make it happen.

In the Canada of the 1980s, once you've paid your dues at King and Bay – you're paid up anywhere.

Hockey, eh?

Trent Frayne

Hockey, eh?

All right, what the historians have noted is that Canada's remorseless winters have forged in us half-frozen natives a certain fortitude, an endurance, an ingenuity for survival. As has been noted by that tiny, dark-haired person with the towering brain, Margaret Atwood, for a Canadian survival is winning.

Except on the battlefield, it's probably true that nowhere is this ingrained characteristic on better view than on the hockey rinks where robust young oafs have been enthusiastically thumping one another for generations, always panting back into the fray for a thump or two more.

Maybe a reason the game is so many people's passion is that we see ourselves in a sudden tableau of Bobby Hull swinging behind the net with the puck, front teeth gone, nose flattened, but fluid as a bird in flight and absolutely full of joy. Or of the other Bobby, Orr, instantly accelerating on his wonky, surgery-saturated knees, exploding into the narrowest of openings. The Bobbys grew up etching icy patterns on the endless flat sweep of the Bay of Quinte and Georgian Bay, absorbing sprains and lumps en route to sports-page immortality.

Anatoli Tarasov, the daddy of Russian hockey (he swiped a lot of his stuff from Toronto's Lloyd Percival who spent years a quarter century ago trying to preach what people now call European-style hockey to indifferent NHL moguls), once noted that the only facet of our style the Sovietskis could never quite duplicate was "the Canadian tenacity." Similarly, Connie Smythe, the grand curmudgeon who founded the Toronto Maple Leafs, was pleased to say the difference between a hockey player and a football player or a baseball player is this: "Hockey guys play if they can breathe."

Then there's Bobby Baun. If it's true that hockey is this particular national trait in microcosm, it follows that nobody better symbolizes it quite like Bobby Baun.

It's the old Detroit Olympia, right? Sixth game, 1964 Stanley Cup final, the Red Wings and the Leafs, the former in front three games to two and the third-period score 3-3. A Detroit win here and it's Good Night Irene.

Baun, a Leaf defenceman with a nose like a road under construction, is nobly defending in front of his goaltender Johnny Bower when Gordie Howe rockets a shot, hoping Baun is screening Bower. It catches Baun's leg just above the ankle. He hears a tiny noise like a firecracker popping.

The puck ricochets to a corner and Baun wheels for it. *Crack!* The bone splits, fire shoots up Baun's leg, he knows it's broken. In the infirmary he impassively has the doctor freeze it and tape it. He goes back out, takes his regular shift and, in overtime, he shoots the winning goal!

Two days pass. Baun stays home on crutches, refusing to visit the club doctor. At the rink for the seventh game he has the leg frozen and plays every shift. Toronto wins the Stanley Cup. Next day, x-rays confirm the break. A cast goes on, heel to knee, that stays there half the summer. Hockey, eh?

RECREATION

A hair-raising ride on the midway at Toronto's
Canadian National Exhibition, the oldest and
largest annual exhibition in the world.

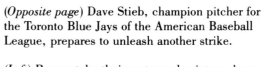

(*Opposite page*) Dave Stieb, champion pitcher for the Toronto Blue Jays of the American Baseball League, prepares to unleash another strike.

(*Left*) Racers take their motorcycles into a sharp turn during the annual Grand Prix races at Mosport.

(*Below*) Carling Bassett, promising young competitor on the international professional tennis circuit, delivers a smashing two-handed backhand shot.

(*Opposite page*) A red-jacketed equestrian takes a jump at a local competition near King City.

(*Left*) A variety of pleasure boats line the harbour in front of Kingston's impressive City Hall, built in 1843 when the city was briefly the capital of Upper Canada.

(*Below*) White-water rafting on the Ottawa River near Beachburg.

(*Below*) With one of Ontario's finest yacht harbours, Belleville is a lovely and prosperous city lying at the mouth of the Moira River on the Bay of Quinte.

(*Bottom*) Upper Canada Village near Morrisburg is a reconstructed pre-1867 village built on the site of the Battle of Crysler's Farm where the British and Americans fought an inconclusive battle during the War of 1812. More than thirty buildings were carefully moved from the St. Lawrence area during construction of the Seaway to recreate Ontario's pioneer past to the last authentic detail.

(*Opposite page*) Gananoque means "place of good health" in Indian, and is right at the heart of the Thousand Islands area.

(*Overleaf*) Ontario Place's geodesic dome is part of a 96-acre playground of extraordinary futuristic structures offering all manner of entertainment. Opened in 1971 off-shore from Toronto's Canadian National Exhibition, it is a popular attraction for both locals and tourists.

(*Opposite page*) Casa Loma, the extravagant dream of financier Sir Henry Pellatt, was built in 1911 at vast cost and now stands like a fairytale castle in the heart of Toronto.

(*Left*) Lions and their cubs gather to feed at the African Lion Safari reserve near Rockton. With over 1000 exotic birds and animals roaming wild, visitors can drive safely through this little bit of Africa.

(*Below*) Near the town of Vaughan north of Toronto, Canada's Wonderland offers an imaginative fantasy park for tourists.

(*Bottom*) A dolphin performs at Niagara Falls' Marineland.

151

(*Opposite page*) Salome Bey sings the blues as Billie Holliday in the award-winning hit *Indigo*, a musical tribute to black music.

(*Below left*) The Toronto Symphony Orchestra tunes up before a performance in the distinctive Roy Thomson Hall, home to the world-famous orchestra.

(*Below right*) Toronto jazz musicians Archie Alleyne and Frank Wright, standing in front of the imaginative Flat Iron Building mural, have developed with their Jazz Quartet a unique sound in Canadian and international jazz.

(*Overleaf*) Veronica Tennant performs an arabesque in a pas de deux with Frank Augustyn, principal dancers with the National Ballet of Canada, during a performance of *Sleeping Beauty* at Toronto's O'Keefe Centre, home to the world-renowned company.

(*Opposite page*) The well-known Canadian actor Heath Lamberts plays Cyrano in the Shaw Festival's critically acclaimed production of *Cyrano de Bergerac*. This annual theatre event in Niagara-on-the-Lake features the plays of George Bernard Shaw and his contemporaries.

(*Left*) The Stratford Shakespearean Festival lies on the lazy, leafy banks of the Avon River. Founded in 1953, the Festival has become an important world theatrical event.

(*Below*) The world-class Canadian Opera Company performs *The Merry Widow* at the O'Keefe Centre.

(*Overleaf*) A warm Ontario sun sets over water and beach in Algonquin Park.